Fearless Freddie

Book #6

A Spirit of Truth Storybook

By Linda Mason

Copyright Page
Fearless Freddie
Book #6

A Spirit of Truth Storybook

Author: Linda C. Mason
Published by: Books By L Mason
P. O. Box 1162
Powhatan, VA 23139
LMasonOnTop@aol.com
www.BooksByLMason.com

ISBN-13: 978-1-62217-741-7
ISBN-10: 1-62217-741-X

© 2014 by Linda C. Mason
 Registration # **TXu 1-925-200**
Illustrated by Jessica Mulles
Edited by Tamara K Mason

Printed in the United States of America.

Fearless Freddie

I'm all grown up now **with** a family

of my own. Among them are my two

boys, Toni and Kelly. Kelly is the

youngest and always cautious and

careful, but Toni, my firstborn, reminds me s**o** much of me as a child. They called me *Fearless Freddie.* I didn't really **u**nderstand why then, but I cer**t**ainly do now.

I grew up on a chicken farm. We raised our chickens to produce eggs that were sold  at the town farmers' market. We had a few pigs as well. Our nearest

neighbor was about a mile away, but it seemed as though most of the children in our small town of Green Pastures always gathered at our farm to play, or should I say, to help me get into all **kin**ds of trouble.

I remember a time when I was around eight years old. Two of my best buddies were over at our farm helping me do my chores. It was a very hot, muggy day in August, and I couldn't

wait to finish my chores so that we

could go down to the pond and pick on the giant snapping turtle that seemed to think it owned the pond.

None of my friends would go anywhere near the pond unless I were with them. Antonio, my friend from school, used to play at the pond, too, but he ended up getting his little finger caught in that old snapping turtle's mouth one day. Now Antonio only has four fingers on one hand.

That kind of thing would have never happened if I had gone down to the pond with him because I knew how to out trick that old turtle. I was

quick, too. Nope! I wasn't afraid of

anything, and everyone knew it.

Today, we all decided to see who

could get the closest to the turtle

before it tried to snap at us. After my

chores were finished, we all strolled down to the pond with our imaginary swords in hand. We were armed and ready to defeat our enemy -- that meant the old turtle that my friends started calling '*Snappy.*'

"March, March, March!" I yelled as we headed through the woods, crunching leaves beneath our feet, as we pressed onward. The sun was still overhead, but there was a cool breeze blowing that made it just right for a mischievous afternoon. I always knew where the turtle would be hiding, so I came up with a plan.

We'd throw rocks at him until he made his way out of the water, hissing and snapping at everyone. Then we would take turns distracting his head while the others tagged him on the back and then ran off. Of course, I was always the first to take my turn, being

the bravest and the most fearless. I

would show the others that there was

nothing to fear, and then I would egg

them on to follow my lead.

Through the years, old Snappy finally stopped hissing at us and started allowing us to pat him on his shell. I loved feeling the bumpy, hard shell, and examining the beautiful green, black, and yellow designs. Sometimes, he would even let us touch his hooked nose as well. It was no longer fun and mischievous anymore, so we eventually just left him alone. Thinking back now, that

was probably old Snappy's plan all along.

Remembering my childhood was one thing, but seeing that fearlessness in my own son now was really strange. Back when I was little, picking on Snappy or tying a rope to a tree branch and swinging from tree to tree like Tarzan were just a few of my daring tricks. Now, twenty years later, away from Green Pastures and old Snappy, the chickens and pigs have been replaced by horses on my own ranch.

My family has settled quite nicely into our two-story farmhouse, and we often spend time outdoors. Toni is six

years old now and has been riding horses since before he could talk. On one particular day, my dreams of random home-improvement projects were replaced by anxiety, as I found myself in the emergency department of a hospital, waiting for the doctors to X-ray Toni's leg.

No, Toni didn't fall off a horse. He

jumped out of a second-story window.

Oh yes -- the second story window of

our own home. You see, he was

playing Superman and wanted to try

out his *'flying skills.'* Early this morning, Kelly came running into my bedroom screaming, that Toni was hurt. I thought they were both in their bedroom, so I headed in that direction. Kelly quickly corrected me and told me to follow him down the stairs and, outside, which puzzled me, but he seemed to know where he was headed.

We ran to the side of the house,

beneath their bedroom window.

There, I saw Toni sitting on the ground

in a huff, dressed in his pajamas with his mom's apron tied around his neck.

"Dad, I was trying to fly like Superman!" He said with a scowl on his face.

"I jumped out of the window, and I was gonna' fly, but this stupid cape is broken," Toni explained, pointing to the apron around his neck.

"Why didn't it work, Dad?!" Toni exclaimed as he began to cry.

"You what?!" I replied in shock and with much concern. After I checked his leg, which was twisted in a strange position, I wondered if my little daredevil would be just as fearless at the hospital when the doctors patched him up. I gave Toni a big hug and assured him that everything would be fine. I smiled at my courageous son as I helped him into the car,

remembering when I was his age. I

probably would have blamed the cape,

too.

Later that evening, as we left the

hospital with Toni's leg in a light blue

cast, I noticed that his tears had dried

and were replaced by a smirk, as I was

sure he was already planning his next

adventure. All of the nurses and doctors, plus a few friends Toni had made while sitting in the waiting room, had autographed his cast.

Toni couldn't wait to get to school to see how many funny remarks he would get when the kids saw his 'trophy.' I guess that talk we had on the way to the hospital about the difference between real life and

television situations didn't quite sink

in.

As I watched him admire his cast, I

wondered how the rest of his

childhood would play out, with so

many more dangerous and wild adventures just waiting to be discovered by my own little superhero -- *Toni, The Invincible*! I took a deep breath, glanced toward the sky, and said, "Lord, somehow, I survived my childhood. Please give me the strength to survive Toni's!"

The End

A special inspirational message has been coded throughout each story to help create *added focus*, as well as a visual tool for interactive participation and concentration.

Decode your secret message and send it to me, along with your name and age, through my personal email address at LMasonOnTop@aol.com, and you will receive a personal email response from me. An Editor's Edition of this 26 Storybook Series is forthcoming, which will include the 26 stories within two complete volumes; at which time, the Master's List of every inspirational message will be revealed.

A Message of Encouragement Worksheet

(You may copy this page)
(Fill in the missing letters on a <u>separate sheet of paper</u> or here, if you own the storybook, to unlock your secret message)

Fearless Freddie

_ i t _ _ _ _   _ _ k _ _ _   r _ _ _ ,

_ _ _ _ _   c _ _   _ _   n _   g _ _ _ _ _ .

J _ _ _   _ _ a _ _   _ _   _ _ k _

c _ l _ u _ _ t _ d   _ _ _ k   _ _ _   _ s _

w _ _ _ _ _ .

* The meaning of the word "risk" = taking chances.
* The meaning of the word "calculated" = to expect a definite outcome.

Spirit of Truth Storybook
Activity Page

1. *After reading the story, ask yourself*

    the following questions:

- What did you like about the story?
- What would you change about the story?
- What could you have done to make things turn out differently?
- Can you think of a way to help others after reading this story?

2. *Go back through the story pages and* **decode** *your* **secret message**.

- Write the message on **the provided worksheet**.
- Send it to me through email at:

    LMasonOnTop@aol.com

I will send you back a personal comment. Be sure to include your gender and age.

3. Cut out the finger puppets and assemble as instructed. Be careful with your scissors.

- Use your finger to help the character walk out a happy scene that you create.

- When finished playing, place your puppet characters in a zip lock bag or an envelope, and store it between your favorite pages of the book for safekeeping.

- Ask your parent or guardian if you can collect all 26 "Spirit of Truth Storybook Series" and remember to save the *Dove Cutouts* and glue them into the proper places on the chart.

Instructions for Making Finger Puppets

1. Cut figures out. Cut around the figure

2. Cut strips out. Follow dotted line.

3. Fold over strip and tape into a ring.

33

4.   **Tape ring on the back of the figure that you cut out.**

Cut out and the Finger Puppets

Cut out the Finger Puppets

Receive a *15% discount coupon* off of the purchase of my Editor's Edition of "**The Spirit of Truth**" Storybook Series, with proof of purchase from A - Z. This special edition will contain all 26 stories within two volumes along with some added goodies. Fill out the chart below and **please print** all the information clearly.

A	B	C	D	E	F
G	H	I	J	K	L
M	N	O	P	Q	R
S	T	U	V	W	X
Y	Z				

Glue your "*Dove Letter*" cutouts in the corresponding boxes, on top of the proper letter. Fill 26 spaces from A-Z. Then cut this page out and mail it to:

Linda Mason
P. O Box 1162
Powhatan, VA 23139

Name _____

Address_____

State: _____ **Zip**_____

Email

Address_____

Dove Letter Cutout

Spirit of Truth Storybook Series

APPROPRIATE AGE LEVEL

COLOR CODING KEY

The reading level for these stories is grade 5, but they can be understood and enjoyed by the ages listed below, sometimes needing to be read to by someone older.

Ages 4 and 5 = GREEN

Ages 6 and 7 = BLUE

Ages 8 and 9 = ORANGE

Ages 10 and above = RED

*A unique inspirational message has been coded throughout each story to help create 'added focus,' as well as a visual tool for interactive concentration. **Decode your secret message (written in red lettering throughout the story)** and send it to me, along with your name and age, through my* *email address on my website, www.BooksByLMason.com, and you will receive a personal email response from me. Some of the letters of the secret message have already been provided to assist you in your decoding. Additionally, added bonuses of finger puppet activities, brain games, puzzles, or other goodies, awaits each reader in the back of every storybook. A delightful "Treasure Hunt" can be found throughout the illustrations from my collection of storybooks, which **details can only be found on my website.***

Also, E-Book Editions of this collection of storybooks, having no activities in the back of the books, as well as A Collector's Edition of this 26 Storybook Series is forthcoming. The collector's edition will include all 26 stories in two volumes, at which time, the Master's List of every inspirational message will be revealed.

Synopsis of Each Story from A-Z

1. *Anxious Arlene:* This story is about a set of rambunctious siblings who live with their loving grandparents, and an adorable, adopted mutt experiencing a few mishaps. This story is recommended for ages five and up.

2. *Busy Benny:* Benny is a dynamic little boy who loves to tinker with wacky car models. He enters a neighborhood race one day with an impressive, wacky race car designed by himself, with the help of his parents. It's also a story about friendship. This story is recommended for ages seven and up.

3. *Catty Carla:* This story is told through the eyes of cats and deal with one cat in particular, with a "Catty" attitude. The insults are released upon another cat that

has a severe physical illness. The gossiper soon regrets the spiteful attitude and adjusts her behavior before the very sick cat transitions to "Kitty Heaven." The story does deal with the death of a pet gracefully. This story is recommended for ages five and up.

4. *Doubtful Denise:* A divorced father is raising his bi-racial daughter, who, at the moment, is full of self-doubt and lacks confidence in her ability to complete any assigned task. Through the love of her father and some very positive friends, Denise learns to believe in herself eventually. This story is recommended for ages seven and up.

5. *Excited Ernesto:* This story is about an average teen who has a fear of riding Roller Coasters. With the help of some of his friends, who also have that same fear, they work through it all at the county fair. This story is recommended for ages seven and up.

6. *Fearless Freddie:* A little boy who loves taking a risk, reminds his father of himself when he was young. Freddie went too far one day and ended up with a severe injury, but will this stop his risky behavior or give

him new ideas to participate in more dangerous stunts? This story is recommended for ages five and up.

7. *Graceful Gregory:* This story highlights the life of a young male teen who has been hassled at school because he loves creative dancing instead of football. Even his football-loving dad sometimes doesn't understand Gregory's love of ballet, jazz, and the many other facets of creative dance. One day, Gregory and his dad worked things out with the help of a teen friend who learns to appreciate the physical strength and courage it takes to become a great dancer. This story is recommended for ages seven and up, but younger if the child is already dancing.

8. *Hopeful Henry:* This story is one example of how staying "hopeful" even through rough times, always pays off. This story is recommended for ages seven and up.

9. *Itchy Irvin:* This story plays out through a pack of dog characters who encounters a little boy with a physical problem that resembles that of his own. The dog and the little boy meets, and beautiful things begin

to happen. This story is recommended for ages seven and up.

10. *Jumping Josey:* This story is about a young teen who lives a life of thrills as a cheerleader. Her hobby takes her into the arena of skydiving. This new adventure eventually leads her to a career in the Armed forces. This story is recommended for ages seven and up.

11. *Kissing Kirkland:* A very "Cutesy" story about a little boy who is infatuated with kissing every animal he comes around, including bugs. This story can is recommended for children ages five and up. This story is recommended for ages five and up.

12. *Lonely Lucilia:* This story deals with teen friendships and having to separate due to a parent's job relocation from one country to another: England to the USA. You can survive when your heart has been broken, even as a child. This story is recommended for ages eight and up.

13. *Muddy Maria:* This story tracks the life of two little girls who loved to play in the mud

as children. This love of "dirty play" eventually led them to a lucrative child business dealing with plants. This story is recommended for ages five and up.

14. *Noisy Nelly:* This story is told through the eyes of a bird who learns, by the wisdom of its mother, that life is much more than things perceived as "gloomy." When you learn to see things from a different perspective, you can soar. This story is recommended for ages seven and up.

15. *Orphaned Ophelia:* Most of this story takes place in a very unique orphanage where several unrelated girls experience different lonely situations, as they all long to be adopted by a family they can call their own. Travel with Ophelia through ups and down in an exciting but lonely place where sometimes there are happy endings. This story is recommended for children ages five and up.

16. *Pudgy Pete:* This story intertwines the life of a slightly plump teen boy with self-esteem issues and an enthusiastic teen girl who just moved in next door. She happens to use a wheelchair. Through the interactions of

these two individuals, Pete's self-esteem takes on a new course, and he learns to see himself more than a plus pants size. This story is recommended for children ages seven and up.

17. *Quarrelsome Quaniqua:* This story contains **sensitive** material, and is not intended to be read as a *bedtime* story. It deals with an abusive living environment (non-sexual but very much physical abuse). Some hard times are happening; however, Quaniqua does figure out, with the help of some new friends, how to turn her situation around. This story is recommended for children eight and up; however, please use parental wisdom as to if this story is suited for your particular child.

18. *Reckless Ricardo:* This story is about a young boy experiencing a reckless, behavioral unbalance due to a peanut allergy. A doctor didn't detect this. In searching the internet, one day, his grandmother (his caretaker) discovers the real issue of dealing with Ricardo. Through a creative experiment, she was able to steer Ricardo's behavior in a

more positive direction. This story can be enjoyed by children ages seven and up.

19. *Shy Stanley:* This story gives you a glimpse into the life of a tranquil little boy who has a unique talent. He channels his energy into drawing. He eventually meets a young girl who has similar skills, and they soon develop a quiet bond. This story can be enjoyed by children ages seven and up.

20. *Tearful Tanya*: This story deals with a little girl who is full of grief over the passing of her grandmother. The family has a spiritual upbringing, and Tanya's mom guides her through the grieving process as she draws strength from above, where she's convinced her grandmother now resides. This story may be a little sensitive if you are a child in a similar situation, yet it can be enjoyed by children ages five and above.

21. *Ungrateful Ursula*: This story contains 'sensitive' material and is recommended for children ages ten and above. Ursula has become accustomed to using "Cutting" to cope with her many issues of life. Walk with her as she moves from "much pain" to

"much gain." She eventually discovers a better way of coping with adversity with the help of her once absent father.

22. *Valiant Vivica*: This story is about a very gifted little girl who loves contact sports to the point of joining a coed wrestling team. Her life is interrupted by a tornado during a wrestling tournament at school. This experience changes her overall focus; however, she remains a top athlete in anything she chooses to pursue even though her aspirations have changed. This story can be enjoyed by children ages eight and above.

23. *Worrying Winston*: If you enjoy treasure hunts, you will love this story. Winston lives with his father while his mom serves in the Marine Armed Forces. They have a unique family unit, but one day Winston's worries come to pass when he gets news from the Armed Forces concerning a severe injury involving his mom. This situation changes their entire world. However, they survive. This story can be enjoyed by children ages eight and above.

24. *X-Con Xavier*: This person is a teen who had to be incarcerated due to destructive behavior caused by a rebellious attitude. Having had an unstable home environment, he had a "So What" attitude. While incarcerated, he encounters an individual that offers him a more positive way of life. What choice will he make? This story is recommended for children ages ten and above.

25. *Yearning Yolanda*: This story gives you a bit of insight through the mind of a young girl who is now blind but wasn't born blind. Walk with Yolanda through an even more formidable challenge as she saves her mother's life during a house fire. Yes, even though she is blind. This story can be enjoyed by children ages eight and above.

26. *Zealous Zeporah*: Zeporah is a very passionate young lady full of enthusiasm for life. She is also a junior coach for her track team at school. She gets injured before a vital track met but never missed a step in leading her team to the most outstanding scores they have ever achieved. This story

can be enjoyed by children ages seven and above.

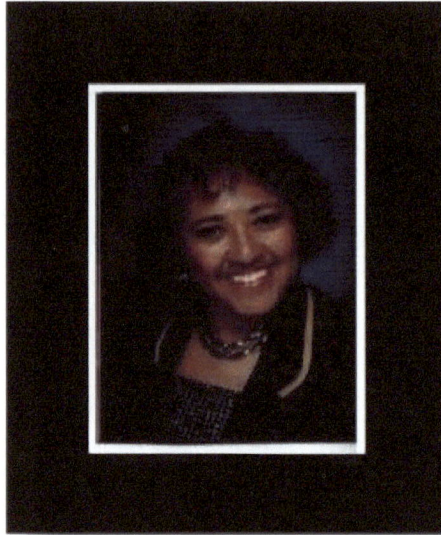

About The Author

Minister Linda Mason is a unique ministry gift to the Body of Christ. Her experiences include the establishment of *Spirit of Praise Liturgical Outreach, Inc.*, a non-profit 501 © three organization, which not only helped to establish and oversee new dance ministries but also extended into the communities.

In addition to the *Spirit of Truth Storybook Series*, Minister Linda has published *Appetizers from the Word of God, Are You Hungry?* Volumes 1, 2, & 3, which is an excellent tool for teaching foundational truths, simplistically, from God's Word.

Linda is a native of Suffolk, Virginia, the wife of George B. Mason, Jr., the mother of three: Tamara, Tiena, and George III. She has three adorable grandchildren; Niyah, Laana, and Aaron. Linda holds an Associate Degree in Early Childhood Education and has a passion for writing. She has published 26 children's stories from A to Z, in addition to over 50 other books, including five suspense teen novels. Linda plans to have these unique stories available in both English and Spanish soon.

What others have stated about this Series

- *Author Linda Mason's book, "Kissing Kirkland," is one of a series of books that tells a delightful story with a secret hidden valuable message for children. Her stories will captivate her audience with a variety of age-appropriate activities to enhance each child's learning. As an educator for many years, I highly recommend her books!* **By Amelia Hopkins, a high school counselor.**

- *Linda Mason has done an excellent job using her creativity and insight in writing this series of books, the **Spirit of Truth Storybook Series from A-Z**. Each book deals with a subject or situation, such as a particular disability or set-back that a child might encounter and have difficulty dealing with. The books offer resolutions that* *are positive and encouraging, helping a child build strength, confidence, and maturity. The activities in the back of each book reinforce the lesson learned. The graphics are colorful and eye-catching, and each book's vocabulary is age-appropriate. Each book is color-coded to fit each age group, so there are appropriate books for every child's age. These are books your children will want to read or hear over and over, read by a big sister or brother. And they also have the opportunity to communicate with the author directly! I highly recommend these books for your children and grandchildren!*

By Nona J. Mason, a retired teacher, mother, and grandmother.

www.ingramcontent.com/pod-product-compliance
Lightning Source LLC
Chambersburg PA
CBHW042124080426
42733CB00002B/11